U.S. Citizenship Test
English Edition
100 Questions and Answers
Includes a Flash Card Format
for Easy Practice

Copyright 2011 © Lakewood Publishing
an imprint of Learning Visions

Please note: Copyright is not claimed for any part of
the original work prepared by the U.S. Government or by
a U.S. state officer or employee as part of that person's official
duties However, such works together with all materials contained
herein, are subject to the preceding copyright notice as to their
compilation and organization in this book Also, although the
materials here represent the best information available and
known to the author to date of publication, no claims are
made as to its continuing accuracy and no guarantees
or claims are made to readers for results based on
using these materials.

U.S. Citizenship Test
English Edition
100 Questions and Answers
Includes a Flash Card Format for Easy Practice
Published by Lakewood Publishing
1710 Moorpark Rd., Suite #213
Thousand Oaks, CA 91360

ISBN: 978-1-936583-04-1
Library of Congress Control Number: 2011930436

1. Citizenship, United States, America, U.S. 2. naturalization, citizenship
3. immigration, citizenship test, new test
4 English – language 5. United States – civics, government, history
6. United States – USCIS new test October 2008
I. Citizenship, American II. Title

Printed in the United States of America

U.S. Citizenship Test
(English Edition)
100 Questions and Answers
Includes a Flash Card Format
for Easy Practice

J.S. Aaron

Available Online:

Translation Software:

www.googletranslate.com
www.babelfish.com

(These can be helpful, but they do not give perfect
translations. They are best used with single words or
simple sentences.)

USCIS Citizenship Information:

www.uscis.com
www.welcomeesl.com

Also Available from Lakewood Publishing

Guide for New Immigrants: *Welcome to the United States*
ISBN: 978-1-936583-42-3 (paperback)
ISBN: 978-1-936583-18-8 (ebook)

Guía para inmigrantes nuevos Bienvenidos a los Estados Unidos
de América
ISBN: 978-1-936583-43-0 (paperback)

USA Citizenship Interview and Test Practice Made Easy
ISBN: 978-1-936583-25-6 (paperback)

*Learn About the United States: Quick Civics Lessons for the
New NaturalizationTest
ISBN: 978-1-936583-01-0 (hardback)
ISBN: 978-0-9793538-1-9 (paperback)
ISBN 978-0-9793538-9-5 (digital/ebook)

U.S. Citizenship Test Questions in 5 Languages--English,
Spanish, Chinese, Tagalog and Vietnamese
English -Español - 中英 - Tagalog - tiếng Việt
ISBN: 978-1-936583-11-9 (hardback)
ISBN: 978-1-936583-10-2 (paperback)

*U.S. Citizenship Test (English edition): 100 Questions and
Answers Includes a Flash Card Format for Easy Practice
ISBN: 978-1-936583-04-1

*U.S.Citizenship Test (English and Spanish - Español y Inglés)
100 Bilingual Questions and Answers 100 Preguntas y
respuestas del exámen de la ciudadanía (2011-2012)
ISBN: 978-1-936583-07-2

US Citizenship Test (Chinese-English 中英) 100 Bilingual
Ques-tions and Answers 新版公民入籍歸化考試的 100 道考題與
答案
ISBN: 978-1-936583-05-8

Table of Contents

Preparing for the U.S. Citizenship Interview

Every year, thousands of people from all over the world become citizens of the United States. American citizenship can give you many new opportunities, but it is not a quick process. It usually takes over ten years to become an American citizen.

The 4 Parts of the Citizenship Interview

The USCIS (United States Citizenship and Immigration Services) is responsible for processing citizenship applications. A USCIS officer (interviewer) will ask you to do four things during your citizenship interview:

1. **Speak and Understand Basic English**. The USCIS officer will ask you questions about your N-400 citizenship application form. These will be questions about your life, work, family, reasons for becoming a citizen, and any problems with the information on your application.

He will also ask questions to be sure that you have been honest, and that you are qualified to become an American citizen.

2. **Read English**. The USCIS officer will ask you to read 1 out of 3 sentences correctly in English. The USCIS does not tell which sentences they use on this test. But they have published a list of recommended reading vocabulary. This list is included in this book beginning on page 45.

3. **Write English.** The USCIS officer will also ask you to write 1 out of 3 sentences correctly in English. He will read a sentence to you, then you will write it down. The USCIS does

not tell which sentences the interviewers will use in the writing test. But they recommend vocabulary words that can be helpful for you to know. These are listed in this book, beginning on page 49.

4. **Know U.S. Civics.** You will also be asked questions about U.S history and government (also called "civics"). The USCIS publishes a list of all of these questions. All 100 civics questions and answers are listed in this book, beginning on page 13. To make them easier to practice, they are also formatted as flashcards, beginning on page 59.

There are 100 civics questions on the USCIS list. You can be asked to answer 10 of these 100 questions in your citizenship interview. When you answer 6 out of 10 questions correctly, you pass the civics test.

The civics questions and answers will all be given orally. You will not be asked to read or write any of your answers to the civics questions.

Bilingual Books Available

The four other books in this *US Citizenship Test* series are all bilingual. They are all formatted to make the information easier to study in English with translations in four different languages.

If you are 65 years old and have been a Permanent Resident for 20 years or more, you can take the civics test in your native language instead of English. These four bilingual books list all 20 questions in a separate section, which makes studying them easier for Permanent Residents who know Spanish, Chinese, Vietnamese or Tagalog.

Of course, bilingual books can also be helpful to people who want to take the civics test in English. Some of the civics vocabulary and concepts will be unfamiliar, even if you know English well. Reading unfamiliar questions and answers in your native language can make it faster to understand and remember the information when you read it in English.

Other Reference Materials

The civics questions and answers that begin on page 13 are the only information that you need to know for the civics test.

But if you would like to read more about any of these questions, you can read the longer USCIS answers in the book, *Learn About the United States: Quick Civics Lessons for the New Naturalization Test* (Lakewood Publishing/Learning Visions).

You will not be tested on the extra information in *Learn About the United States*. But the longer readings can help you understand why these 100 questions are so important for all American citizens to know. They are also a good way to practice your reading skills and improve your vocabulary, especially in U.S. history, geography, and government.

To help you prepare for all parts of your citizenship test, there are also free citizenship study materials and a link to a sample USCIS video interview online at:

www.welcomeesl.com or **www.uscis.gov**

Becoming a U.S. citizen can be a wonderful, life-changing experience. We encourage you on your journey to citizenship and look forward to welcoming you as a new American citizen.

Introduction to the Civics Test Questions (from USCIS)

Civics (History and Government) Questions for the Redesigned (New) Naturalization Test

The 100 civics (history and government) questions and answers for the citizenship (naturalization) test are listed below.

Applicants who filed the Application for Naturalization, Form N-400, on or after October 1, 2008, should study this list. The civics test is an oral test and the USCIS Officer will ask the applicant up to 10 of the 100 civics questions.

An applicant must answer 6 out of 10 questions correctly to pass the civics portion of the naturalization test.

Although USCIS knows that there may be additional correct answers to the 100 civics questions, applicants are encouraged to use the answers provided below.

Note: For those 65 years old and older. *If you are 65 years old or older and have been a legal permanent resident of the United States for 20 or more years, you may study just the questions that have been marked with an asterisk at the end of each question. (*) .

These 20 questions for people 65 years and older are also listed separately on page 39.

100 Civics Questions and Answers

American Government

A: Principles of American Democracy

1. What is the supreme law of the land?

   the Constitution

2. What does the Constitution do? (know one)

   - sets up the government
   - defines the government
   - protects basic rights of Americans

3. The idea of self-government is in the first three words of the Constitution. What are these words?

   We the People

4. What is an amendment?

   - a change (to the Constitution)
   - an addition (to the Constitution)

5. What do we call the first ten amendments to the Constitution?

   The Bill of Rights

6. What is <u>one</u> right or freedom from the First Amendment?*
    - speech
    - religion
    - assembly
    - press
    - petition the government

7. How many amendments does the Constitution have?

    twenty-seven (27)

8. What did the Declaration of Independence do?

    - announced our independence (from Great Britain)
    - declared our independence (from Great Britain)
    - said that the United States is free (from Great Britain)

9. What are two rights in the Declaration of Independence?

    - life
    - liberty
    - pursuit of happiness

10. What is freedom of religion?

    You can practice any religion, or not practice (have) a religion.

11. What is the economic system in the United States?*

- capitalist economy
- market economy

12. What is the "rule of law"?

- Everyone must follow the law.
- Leaders must obey the law.
- Government must obey the law.
- No one is above the law.

B: System of Government

13. Name one branch or part of the government.*

- Congress
- legislative
- President
- executive
- the courts
- judicial

14. What stops one branch of government from becoming too powerful?

- checks and balances
- separation of powers

15. Who is in charge of the executive branch?

the President

15

16. Who makes federal laws?

   - Congress
   - Senate and House (of Representatives)
   - (U.S. or national) legislature

17. What are the two parts of the U.S. Congress?*

   the Senate and House (of Representatives)

18. How many U.S. Senators are there?

   one hundred (100)

19. We elect a U.S. Senator for how many years?

   six (6)

20. Who is one of your state's U.S. Senators now?*

   ▪ Answers will be different for each state. Check the internet **www.senate.gov** for the current names in your state.
   [District of Columbia residents and residents of U.S. territories should answer that D.C. (or the territory where the applicant lives) has no U.S. Senators.]

21. The House of Representatives has how many voting members?

   four hundred thirty-five (435)

22. We elect a U.S. Representative for how many years?

two (2)

23. Name your U.S. Representative.

▪ Answers will be different for each area. See the website: **www.house.gov** for the newest names.

[Residents of territories with non-voting Delegates or Resident Commissioners may provide the name of that Delegate or Commissioner. Also acceptable is any statement that the territory has no (voting) Representatives in Congress.]

24. Who does a U.S. Senator represent?

all people of the state

25. Why do some states have more Representatives than other states?

- (because of) the state's population
- (because) they have more people
- (because) some states have more people

26. We elect a President for how many years?

four (4)

27. In what month do we vote for President?*

November

28. What is the name of the President of the United States now?*

  - Barack Obama
  - Obama

29. What is the name of the Vice President of the United States now?

  - Joseph R. Biden, Jr.
  - Joe Biden
  - Biden

30. If the President can no longer serve, who becomes President?

  the Vice President

31. If both the President and the Vice President can no longer serve, who becomes President?

  the Speaker of the House

32. Who is the Commander in Chief of the military?

  the President

33. Who signs bills to become laws?

  the President

34. Who vetoes bills?

  the President

35. **What does the President's Cabinet do?**

advises the President

36. **What are two Cabinet-level positions?**

- Vice President
- Attorney General
- Secretary of Agriculture
- Secretary of Commerce
- Secretary of Defense
- Secretary of Education
- Secretary of Energy
- Secretary of Health and Human Services
- Secretary of Homeland Security
- Secretary of Housing and Urban Development
- Secretary of the Interior
- Secretary of Labor
- Secretary of State
- Secretary of Transportation
- Secretary of the Treasury
- Secretary of Veterans Affairs

37. **What does the judicial branch do?**

- reviews laws
- explains laws
- resolves disputes (disagreements)
- decides if a law goes against the Constitution

38. **What is the highest court in the United States?**

the Supreme Court

39. How many justices are on the Supreme Court?

nine (9)

40. Who is the Chief Justice of the United States now? (Know one way to say his name).

- John Roberts
- John G. Roberts, Jr.

41. Under our Constitution, some powers belong to the federal government. What is one power of the federal government?

- to print money
- to declare war
- to create an army
- to make treaties

42. Under our Constitution, some powers belong to the states. What is one power of the states?

- provide schooling and education
- provide protection (police)
- provide safety (fire departments)
- give a driver's license
- approve zoning and land use

43. Who is the Governor of your state now?

- Answers will be different for each state. [District of Columbia residents should answer that D.C. does not have a Governor.]

44. What is the capital of your state?*

The States and the State Capitals

Alabama - Montgomery
Alaska - Juneau
Arizona - Phoenix
Arkansas - Little Rock
California - Sacramento
Colorado - Denver
Connecticut - Hartford
Delaware - Dover
Florida - Tallahassee
Georgia - Atlanta
Hawaii - Honolulu
Idaho - Boise
Illinois - Springfield
Indiana - Indianapolis
Iowa - Des Moines
Kansas - Topeka
Kentucky - Frankfort
Louisiana - Baton Rouge
Maine - Augusta
Maryland - Annapolis
Massachusetts - Boston
Michigan - Lansing
Minnesota - St. Paul
Mississippi - Jackson
Missouri - Jefferson City
Montana - Helena

Nebraska - Lincoln
Nevada - Carson City
New Hampshire - Concord
New Jersey - Trenton
New Mexico - Santa Fe
New York - Albany
North Carolina - Raleigh
North Dakota - Bismarck
Ohio - Columbus
Oklahoma - Oklahoma City
Oregon - Salem
Pennsylvania - Harrisburg
Rhode Island - Providence
South Carolina - Columbia
South Dakota - Pierre
Tennessee - Nashville
Texas - Austin
Utah - Salt Lake City
Vermont - Montpelier
Virginia - Richmond
Washington - Olympia
West Virginia - Charleston
Wisconsin - Madison
Wyoming - Cheyenne

[District of Columbia residents should answer that D.C. is not a state and does not have a capital. Residents of U.S. territories should name the capital of the territory.]

45. What are the two major political parties in the United States?*

Democratic and Republican

46. What is the political party of the President now?

Democratic (Party)

47. What is the name of the Speaker of the House of Representatives now?

(John) Boehner

C: Rights and Responsibilities

48. There are four amendments to the Constitution about who can vote. Describe one of them.

- Citizens eighteen (18) and older (can vote).
- You don't have to pay (a poll tax) to vote.
- Any citizen can vote. (Women and men can vote.)
- A male citizen of any race (can vote).

49. What is one responsibility that is only for United States citizens?*

- serve on a jury;
- vote in a federal election

50. Name one right only for United States citizens.

     - vote in a federal election
     - run for federal office

51. What are <u>two</u> rights of everyone living in the United States?

- freedom of expression   - freedom of worship
- freedom of speech   - the right to bear arms
- freedom of assembly
- freedom to petition the government

52. What do we show loyalty to when we say the Pledge of Allegiance?

     - the United States
     - the flag

53. What is one promise you make when you become a United States citizen?

     - to give up loyalty to other countries
     - to defend the Constitution and laws of the
          United States
     - to obey the laws of the United States
     - to serve in the U.S. military (if needed)
     - to serve (do important work for) the nation (if
          needed)
     - to be loyal to the United States

54. How old do citizens have to be to vote for President?*

eighteen (18) and older

55. What are two ways that Americans can participate in their democracy?

- vote
- join a political party
- help with a campaign
- join a civic group
- join a community group
- give an elected official your opinion on an issue
- call Senators and Representatives
- publicly support or oppose an issue or policy
- run for office write to a newspaper

56. When is the last day you can send in federal income tax forms?*

April 15

57. When must all men register for the Selective Service?

- at age eighteen (18)
- between eighteen (18) and twenty-six (26)

The Selective Service

American History

A: Colonial Period and Independence

58. What is one reason colonists came to America?

- freedom
- political liberty
- religious freedom
- economic opportunity
- practice their religion
- escape persecution

59. Who lived in America before the Europeans arrived?

- American Indians
- Native Americans

60. What group of people was taken to America and sold as slaves?

- Africans
- people from Africa

61. Why did the colonists fight the British?

- because of high taxes ("taxation without representation")
- because the British army stayed in their - houses (boarding, quartering)
- because they didn't have self-government

62. Who wrote the Declaration of Independence?

(Thomas) Jefferson

63. When was the Declaration of Independence adopted?

July 4, 1776

64. There were 13 original states. Name <u>three</u>.

Connecticut
Delaware
Georgia
Maryland
Massachusetts
New Hampshire
New Jersey
New York
North Carolina
Pennsylvania
Rhode Island
South Carolina
Virginia

65. What happened at the Constitutional Convention?

- The Constitution was written.
- The Founding Fathers wrote the
        Constitution.

66. When was the Constitution written?

1787

67. The Federalist Papers supported the passage of the U.S. Constitution. Name one of the writers.

- (James) Madison
- (Alexander) Hamilton
- (John) Jay
- Publius

68. What is one thing Benjamin Franklin is famous for?

- U.S. diplomat
- oldest member of the Constitutional
        Convention
- first Postmaster General of the United States
- writer of "Poor Richard's Almanac"
- started the first free libraries

69. Who is the "Father of Our Country"?

(George) Washington

70. Who was the first President?*

(George) Washington

George Washington,
the First U.S. President

B: The U.S. in the 1800s

71. What territory did the United States buy
from France in 1803?

- the Louisiana Territory
- Louisiana

72. Name <u>one</u> war fought by the United States
in the 1800s.

- War of 1812
- Mexican-American War
- Civil War
- Spanish-American War

73. Name the U.S. war between the North and
the South. (Both are correct ways to say the name
of this war. You need to remember <u>one</u> of them.)

- the Civil War
- the War between the States

74. Name <u>one</u> problem that led to the Civil War.

- slavery
- economic reasons
- states' rights

75. What was <u>one</u> important thing that Abraham Lincoln did?*

-freed the slaves (Emancipation Proclamation)
-saved (or preserved) the Union
-led the United States during the Civil War

Abraham Lincoln,
President during the Civil War

76. What did the Emancipation Proclamation do?

-freed the slaves
-freed slaves in the Confederacy
-freed slaves in the Confederate states
-freed slaves in most Southern states

77. What did Susan B. Anthony do?

-fought for women's rights
-fought for civil rights

C: Recent American History and Other Important Historical
Information

78. Name <u>one</u> war fought by the United States in
the 1900s.*

-World War I
-World War II
-Korean War
-Vietnam War
-(Persian) Gulf War

79. Who was President during World War I?

(Woodrow) Wilson

80. Who was President during the Great
Depression and World War II?

(Franklin) Roosevelt

81. Who did the United States fight in World War II?

Japan, Germany, and Italy

82. Before he was President, Eisenhower was a general. What war was he in?

World War II

83. During the Cold War, what was the main concern of the United States?

Communism

84. What movement tried to end racial discrimination?

civil rights (movement)

85. What did Martin Luther King, Jr. do?*

-fought for civil rights
-worked for equality for all Americans

86. What major event happened on September 11, 2001, in the United States?

-Terrorists attacked the United States.

87. Name <u>one</u> American Indian tribe in the United States.

[USCIS Officers will be supplied with a list of federally recognized American Indian tribes.]

Apache	Inuit
Arawak	roquois
Blackfeet	Lakota
Cherokee	Mohegan
Cheyenne	Navajo
Chippewa	Oneida
Choctaw	Pueblo
Creek	Seminole
Crow	Shawnee
Hopi	Sioux
Huron	Teton

Integrated Civics

A: Geography

88. Name <u>one</u> of the two longest rivers in the United States.

- Mississippi (River)
- Missouri (River)

89. What ocean is on the West Coast of the United States?

Pacific (Ocean)

90. **What ocean is on the East Coast of the United States?**

    Atlantic (Ocean)

91. **Name <u>one</u> U.S. territory.**

    - Puerto Rico
    - U.S. Virgin Islands
    - American Samoa
    - Northern Mariana Islands
    - Guam

92. **Name <u>one</u> state that borders Canada.**

    Alaska   New York
    Idaho   North Dakota
    Maine   Ohio
    Michigan   Pennsylvania
    Minnesota   Vermont
    Montana   Washington
    New Hampshire

93. **Name <u>one</u> state that borders Mexico.**

    - California
    - Arizona
    - New Mexico
    - Texas

94. What is the capital of the United States?*

Washington, D.C.

95. Where is the Statue of Liberty?* (These both mean the same place. Remember <u>one</u> of these.)

- New York (Harbor)
- Liberty Island
[Also acceptable are "New Jersey", "near New York City", or "on the Hudson (River)".]

The Statue of Liberty

B: Symbols

96. Why does the flag have 13 stripes?

- because there were 13 original colonies
- because the stripes represent the original colonies

97. Why does the flag have 50 stars?*

- because there is one star for each state
- because each star represents a state
- because there are 50 states

98. What is the name of the national anthem?

The Star-Spangled Banner

C: Holidays

99. When do we celebrate Independence Day?*

July 4

100. Name __two__ national U.S. holidays.

- New Year's Day

- Martin Luther King, Jr. Day

- Presidents' Day

- Memorial Day

- Independence Day

- Labor Day

- Columbus Day

- Veterans Day

- Thanksgiving

- Christmas

Independence Day, July 4th

"65/20"
The 20 Civics Questions
for People 65 and older

65/20

20 Civics Questions

*If you are 65 years old or older and have been a legal permanent resident of the United States for 20 or more years, you only need to know the questions that have been marked with an asterisk.(*) They are also listed below.

Questions: #6, 11, 13, 17, 20, 27, 28, 44, 45, 49, 54, 56, 70, 75, 78, 85, 94, 95, 97, 99

6. What is one right or freedom from the First Amendment?*

- speech
- religion
- assembly
- press
- petition the government

11. What is the economic system in the United States?*

- capitalist economy
- market economy

13. Name one branch or part of the government.*

- Congress (or legislative)
- President (or executive)
- the courts (or judicial)

17. What are the two parts of the U.S. Congress?*

the Senate and House (of Representatives)

20. Who is one of your state's U.S. Senators now?*

Answers will be different for each state.

[District of Columbia residents and residents of U.S. territories should answer that D.C. (or the territory where the applicant lives) has no U.S. Senators.]

27. In what month do we vote for President?*

November

28. What is the name of the President of the United States now?*

- Barack Obama
- Obama

44. What is the capital of your state?*

Answers will be different by state. See page 99.

[District of Columbia residents should answer that D.C. is not a state and does not have a capital. Residents of U.S. territories should name the capital of the territory.]

45. What are the two major political parties in the United States?*

Democratic and Republican

49. What is one responsibility that is only for United States citizens?*

- serve on a jury
- vote in a federal election
- the flag

54. How old do citizens have to be to vote for President?*

eighteen (18) and older

56. When is the last day you can send in federal income tax forms?*

April 15

70. Who was the first President?*

(George) Washington

75. What was one important thing that Abraham Lincoln did?*

- freed the slaves (Emancipation Proclamation)
- saved (or preserved) the Union
- led the United States during the Civil War

78. **Name one war fought by the United States in the 1900s.***
    - World War I
    - World War II
    - Korean War
    - Vietnam War
    - (Persian) Gulf War

85. **What did Martin Luther King, Jr. do?***

    - fought for civil rights
    - worked for equality for all Americans

94. **What is the capital of the United   States?***

    Washington, D.C.

95. **Where is the Statue of Liberty?***

    - New York (Harbor)
    - Liberty Island

    [Also acceptable are New Jersey, near New York City, and on the Hudson (River).]

97. **Why does the flag have 50 stars?***

    - because there is one star for each state
    - because each star represents a state
    - because there are 50 states

99. **When do we celebrate Independence Day?***

    July 4

The Reading Test

Your reading test will be 1-3 sentences. You must read one (1) of three (3) sentences correctly to show that you can read English. These are the words the USCIS recommends for you to know, but other words may be included.

The sentences will be simple. Remember to capitalize names, dates, titles, and the first letter of the sentence. Remember to put a period at the end of a sentence. Put a question mark at the end of a question.

Reading Vocabulary (USCIS Recommended List)

The USCIS will show you 3 sentences, but you only need to read one (1) correctly. The list below has the basic English words that the USCIS recommends for you to know, but they do not say if these will be on the test. Know these, but also read as much English as you can, including the questions in this book.

Question Words

how
what
when
where
why
who

Other

a
for
here
in
of
on
the
to
we

Verbs

can
come
do/does
elects
have/has
be/is/are/was
lives/lived
meet
name
pay
vote
want

Other

colors
dollar bill
first
largest
many
most
north
one
people
second
south

People	Places
George Washington	America
Abraham Lincoln	United States
	U.S.

Civics	Holidays
American flag	Presidents' Day
Bill of Rights	Memorial Day
capital	Flag Day
citizen	Independence Day
city	Labor Day
Congress	Columbus Day
country	Thanksgiving
Father of Our Country	
government	
President	
right	
Senators	
state/states	
White House	

The Writing Test

Practice tip: Have someone read you sentences with these vocabulary words. Practice writing down sentences as they are dictated (spoken) to you.

Writing Vocabulary (USCIS Recommended List)

You will be read 1-3 short sentences and asked to write them. You must write one (1) out of three (3) sentences correctly. The USCIS (INS) does not tell the words they use on the writing test. These are the words they recommend as the basic vocabulary that you should know, but there may be other words to write on the test, too.

Months

February
September
May
October
June
November
July

People
Adams
Lincoln
Washington

Holidays

Presidents' Day
Columbus Day
Thanksgiving
Flag Day

Civics

American Indian
capital
citizens
Civil War
Congress
Father of Our Country
flag
free
freedom of speech
President
right
Senators
state/states
White House

Labor Day
Memorial Day
Independence Day

Places	Verbs
Alaska	be/is/was
California	can
Canada	come
Delaware	elect
Mexico	have/has
New York City	lives/lived
Washington, D.C.	meets
United States	pay
	vote
	want

Other (content)	Other
blue	one hundred/ 100
dollar bill	people
fifty / 50	red
first	second
largest	south
most	taxes
north	white
one	

Other (Function)	
and	of
during	on
for	the
here	to
in	we

For More Information:
Government Addresses, Websites and Phone Numbers

For More Information

U.S. Government Addresses, Websites, and Phone Numbers

If you don't know where to call, start with
1-800-FED-INFO (or 1-800-333-4636) for more information.
For hard-of- hearing, call 1-800-326-2996.
The government also has a website:
http://www.USA.gov
Go there for general information about government agencies.

Department of Education (ED)
U.S. Department of Education
400 Maryland Avenue SW
Washington, DC 20202
Phone: 1-800-872-5327
For hearing impaired: 1-800-437-0833
http://www.ed.gov

Equal Employment Opportunity Commission (EEOC)
U.S. Equal Employment Opportunity Commission
1801 L Street NW
Washington, DC 20507
Phone: 1-800-669-4000
For hearing impaired: 1-800-669-6820
http://www.eeoc.gov

Department of Health and Human Services (HHS)
U.S. Department of Health and Human Services
200 Independence Avenue SW
Washington, DC 20201
Phone: 1-877-696-6775
http://www.hhs.gov

Department of Homeland Security (DHS)
U.S. Department of Homeland Security
Washington, DC 20528
http://www.dhs.gov

U.S. Citizenship and Immigration Services (USCIS)
Phone: 1-800-375-5283
For hearing impaired: 1-800-767-1833
http://www.uscis.gov

U.S. Customs and Border Protection (CBP)
Phone: 202-354-1000
http://www.cbp.gov

U.S. Immigration and Customs Enforcement (ICE)
http://www.ice.gov

Department of Housing and Urban Development (HUD)
U.S. Department of Housing and Urban Development
451 7th Street SW
Washington, DC 20410
Phone: 202-708-1112
For hearing impaired: 202-708-1455
http://www.hud.gov

Department of Justice (DOJ)
U.S. Department of Justice
950 Pennsylvania Avenue NW
Washington, DC 20530-0001
Phone: 202-514-2000
http://www.usdoj.gov

Internal Revenue Service (IRS)

Phone: 1-800-829-1040

For hearing impaired: 1-800-829-4059

http://www.irs.gov

Selective Service System (SSS)

Registration Information Office

PO Box 94638

Palatine, IL 60094-4638

Phone: 847-688-6888

For hearing impaired: 847-688-2567

http://www.sss.gov

Social Security Administration (SSA)

Office of Public Inquiries

6401 Security Boulevard

Baltimore, MD 21235

Phone: 1-800-772-1213

For hearing impaired: 1-800-325-0778

http://www.socialsecurity.gov or
http://www.segurosocial.gov/espanol/.

Department of State (DOS)

U.S. Department of State

2201 C Street NW

Washington, DC 20520

Phone: 202-647-4000

http://www.state.gov

You Can Also....

Check: **www.welcomeesl.com** for new information and practice materials

Visit the USCIS website at **http://www.uscis.gov**

You can also go to **http://www.welcometousa.gov** -- a government website for new immigrants.

Call **Customer Service** at 1-800-375-5283 or 1-800-767-1833 (hearing impaired).

Get USCIS forms, by calling 1-800-870-3676 or looking on the USCIS website (above)

Libraries also have helpful information, includi3ng books, free CDs, DVDs., and free computers to use.

More Helpful Study Ideas:

1. **Find a class.** Local adult schools and community organizations give citizenship classes. You will learn with a teacher and enjoy meeting people from other countries and cultures.

2. **Read the questions out loud** to a tape recorder or download the podcast) from **www.welcomeesl.com.** (You can also watch the video citizenship interview there.)

3. **Listen to your tape, mp3 or CD often.** The civics test is oral. The more English you hear, the more confident you will be at your test.

Flash Cards

Make flash cards. Then use them to study, practice and review the 100 Civics Questions.

100 Civics Questions
Flash Card Format

Directions:

1. Remove the next pages from this book.

2. Cut each page on the dotted lines

--------------------------- so that you have three
separate cards per page.

3. Keep the cut papers ("flashcards") in an envelope.

4. Practice. Read the question on the front and give the
answer. Then look at the back to see if your answer was
correct.

front

| What is the supreme |
| law of the land? |

back

| The Constitution |

5. Keep the questions that you missed in a separate
group from the questions that you already know the
answers to. Practice the ones you don't know again and
again.

Note: You can cut these questions out to make flash
cards. Or you can practice reading and writing these by
copying them onto the front and back of note cards
(also called "index cards"), then using them to study.

1. What is the supreme (highest)
    law of the land?

<------cut completely across-------->

2. What does the Constitution do?

<------cut completely across-------->

3. The idea of self-government is in the first
    three words of the Constitution.

    What are these words?

1. the Constitution

2. sets up the government

   You need to know one answer.
   For more choices, see page 13.

3. We the People

4. What is an amendment?

- -

5. What do we call the first ten
   amendments to the Constitution?

- -

6. What is one right or freedom
   from the First Amendment?*

4. a change (to the Constitution)

5. the Bill of Rights

6. freedom of religion

You need to know one answer.
For more choices, see page 14.

7. How many amendments does the Constitution have?

- -

8. What did the Declaration of Independence do?

- -

9. What are two rights in the Declaration of Independence?

7. Twenty-seven (27)

8. announced our independence
    (from Great Britain)

    You need to know one answer.
    For more choices, see page 14.

9. -life
    -liberty

    You need to know two rights.
    For more choices, see page 14.

10. What is freedom of religion?

----

11. What is the economic system in the United States?*

----

12. What is the "rule of law"?

10. People can observe (have) any religion or no religion

11. capitalist economy

12. Everyone must follow the law.

You need to know one answer.
For other choices, see page 15.

13. Name one branch or part of
    the government.*

- -

14. What stops one branch of
    government from becoming too
    powerful?

- -

15. Who is in charge of the
    executive branch?

13. Congress

    You need to know one branch.
    For other choices, see page 15.

14. checks and balances

15. the President

16. Who makes federal laws?

- -

17. What are the two parts of the U.S. Congress?*

- -

18. How many U.S. Senators are there?

16. Congress

17. the Senate and House (of
     Representatives)

18. one hundred (100)

19. We elect a U.S. Senator for
     how many years?

- -

20. Who is one of your state's
       U.S. Senators now?*

- -

21. The House of Representatives has how
many voting members?

19. six (6)

20. Answers will differ.

[District of Columbia residents and residents of U.S. territories should answer that D.C. (or the territory where the applicant lives) has no U.S. Senators.]

21. four hundred thirty-five   (435)

22. We elect a U.S. Representative for how many years?

----

23. Name your U.S. Representative.

----

24. Who does a U.S. Senator represent?

22. two (2)

23. *Answers will be different for every state.

Residents of territories with non-voting Delegates or Resident Commissioners may provide the name of that Delegate or Commissioner. Also acceptable is any statement that the territory has no (voting) Representatives in Congress.

24. All the people.

25. Why do some states have more
     Representatives than other states?

----

26. We elect a President for how many
     years?

----

27. In what month do we vote
     for President?*

25. (because) they have more people

    You need to know one answer.
    For other choices, see page 17.

26. four (4)

27. November

28. What is the name of the President of the United States now?*

----

29. What is the name of the Vice President of the United States now?

----

30. If the President can no longer serve, who becomes President?

28. Barack Obama

For other ways to say this,
see page 17

29. Joe Biden

For other ways to say this,
see page 18.

30. the Vice President

31. If both the President and the Vice President can no longer serve, who becomes President?

----

32. Who is the Commander in Chief of the military?

----

33. Who signs bills to become laws?

31. the Speaker of the House

32. the President

33. the President

34. Who vetoes bills?

----

35. What does the President's
    Cabinet do?

----

36. What are two Cabinet-level
    positions?

34. the President

35. advises the President

36. Vice President;
     Secretary of State

     You only need to know 2 positions.
     For other choices, see page 19.

37. What does the judicial branch do?

----

38. What is the highest court in
    the United States?

----

39. How many justices are on the Supreme
    Court?

37. explains laws

     You need to know one answer.
     For other choices, see page 19.

38. the Supreme Court

39. nine (9)

40. Who is the Chief Justice of
     the United States now?

----

41. Under our Constitution, some powers
     belong to the federal government. What
     is one power of the federal government?

----

42. Under our Constitution, some powers
     belong to the states. What is one power
     of the states?

40. John Roberts

41. to declare war

     You need to know one power.
     For other choices, see page 20.

42. to give a driver's license

     You only need to know one power.
     For more choices, see page 20.

43. Who is the Governor of your state now?

----

44. What is the capital of your state?*

----

45. What are the two major political parties in the United States?*

43. Answers will be different

[District of Columbia residents should answer that D.C. does not have a Governor.]

44. Answers will differ--see page 21.

[District of Columbia residents should answer that D.C. is not a state and does not have a capital. Residents of U.S. territories should name the capital of the territory.]

45. Democratic and Republican

46. What is the political party
    of the President now?

- -

47. What is the name of the Speaker of
    the House of Representatives?

- -

48. There are four amendments to the
    Constitution about who can vote.

    Describe one of them.

46. Democratic (Party)

47. (John) Boehner

48. Any U.S. citizen over 18 years old can vote.

    You need to know one amendment. For other choices, see page 22.

49. What is one responsibility that is only for United States citizens?*

- -

50. Name one right only for United States citizens.

- -

51. What are two rights of everyone living in the United States?

49. to serve on a jury

You only need to know one answer.
For other choices, see page 22.

50. to vote in a federal election

51. freedom of religion

You need to know one right.
For more choices, see page 23

52. What do we show loyalty to when we say the Pledge of Allegiance?

----

53. What is one promise you make when you become a United States citizen?

----

54. How old do citizens have to be to vote for President?

52. the United States

53. to defend the U.S.

    You need to know one answer.
    For more choices, see page 23.

54. 18 (eighteen and older)

55. What are two ways that Americans can participate in their democracy?

----

56. When is the last day you can send in federal income tax forms?*

----

57. When must all men register for the Selective Service?

55. (1) vote;
     (2) join a political party

For more choices of answers, see page 24.

56. April 15

57. at age eighteen (18)

58. What is one reason colonists came to America?

- -

59. Who lived in America before the Europeans arrived?

- -

60. What group of people was taken to America and sold as slaves?

58. freedom

    You need to know one reason.
    For more reasons, see page 25.

59. American Indians

    For another way to say it, see page 25.

60. people from Africa

61. Why did the colonists fight
    the British? (1 reason)

- -

62. Who wrote the Declaration
    of Independence?

- -

63. When was the Declaration
    of Independence adopted?

61. because of high taxes
    ("taxation without representation")

    You need to know one answer.
    For other choices, see page 25.

62. (Thomas) Jefferson

63. July 4, 1776

64. There were 13 original states.
    Name three.

----

65. What happened at the
    Constitutional Convention?

----

66. When was the Constitution written?

64. New York
New Jersey
North Carolina

For a complete list, see page 26.

65. The Constitution was written.

For other answers, see page 27.

66. 1787

67. The Federalist Papers supported the passage of the U.S. Constitution. Name one of the writers.

----

68. What is one thing Benjamin Franklin is famous for?

----

69. Who is the "Father of Our Country"?

67. (James) Madison

You need to know one writer.
For other choices, see page 27.

68. He started the first free libraries

You need to know one answer.
For more choices, see page 27.

69. (George) Washington

70. Who was the first President?*

----

71. What territory did the United States
    buy from France in 1803?

----

72. Name one war fought by the
    United States in the 1800s.

70.   (George) Washington

71. Louisiana

For another way to say this,
see page 28.

72. Civil War

You need to know one war.
For more choices, see page 28.

73. Name the U.S. war between the North and the South.

- -

74. Name one problem that led to the Civil War.

- -

75. What was one important thing that Abraham Lincoln did?*

73. the Civil War

For another way to say this,
see page 28.

74. slavery

You need to know one answer.
For other choices, see page 29.

75. freed the slaves

You need to know one answer.
For more choices, see page 29.

76. What did the Emancipation
    Proclamation do?

----

77. What did Susan B. Anthony
    do?

----

78. Name one war fought by the United
    States in the 1900s.*

76. freed the slaves

   You need to know one answer. For
   another choice, see page 29.

77. fought for women's rights

   You need to know one answer. For more
   choices, see page 30.

78. World War I

   You need to know one answer. For more
   choices, see page 30.

79. Who was President during World War I?

- -

80. Who was President during the Great
     Depression and World War II?

- -

81. Who did the United States
     fight in World War II?

79. (Woodrow) Wilson

80. (Franklin) Roosevelt

81. Japan, Germany, and Italy

82. Before he was President Eisenhower
     was a general. What war was he in?

----

83. During the Cold War, what was the
     main concern of the United States?

----

84. What movement tried to end
     racial discrimination?

82. World War II

83. Communism

84. the civil rights movement

85. What did Martin Luther King, Jr. do?*

----

86. What major event happened on September 11, 2001, in the United States?

----

87. Name one American Indian tribe in the United States.

[USCIS Officers will be given a list of recognized American Indian tribes.]

85. He worked for equality for
    all Americans

    You need to know one answer. For
    other ways to answer, see page 31.

86. Terrorists attacked the United States.

87. Pueblo

    You need to know <u>one</u> tribe.
    For more tribes, see page 32.

88. Name one of the two longest rivers in the United States.

- -

89. What ocean is on the West Coast of the United States?

- -

90. What ocean is on the East Coast of the United States?

88. Missouri (River)

You need to know one river.
For the other river, see page 32.

89. Pacific (Ocean)

90. Atlantic (Ocean)

91. Name one U.S. territory.

----

92. Name one state that borders Canada.

----

93. Name one state that borders Mexico.

91. Puerto Rico

You need to know one territory.
To see the complete list, see page 33.

92. Alaska

You need to know one state.
To see the complete list, see page 33.

93. California

You need to know one state.
To see a complete list, see page 33

94. What is the capital of the United States?*

- -

95. Where is the Statue of Liberty?*

- -

96. Why does the flag have 13 stripes?

94. Washington, D.C.

95. New York (Harbor)

   You need to know one answer.
   For other ways to answer, see page 34.

96. because there were 13 original
    colonies

   You need to know one answer.
   For more choices, see page 34.

97. Why does the flag have 50 stars?*

- -

98. What is the name of the
      national anthem?

- -

99. When do we celebrate
      Independence Day?*

97. because there are 50 states

You need to know one answer.
For other ways to say this, see page 34.

98. "The Star-Spangled Banner"

99. July 4

100. Name two national U.S. holidays.

- -

100. -Thanksgiving
    - Christmas

You need to know two holidays.
For the complete list, see page 35.